SECRETS

OF AMERICAN HISTORY

★ SPACE AGE ★

You Can't Bring a Sandwich to the Moon . . .
and Other Stories about Space!

by Laurie Calkhoven
illustrated by Valerio Fabbretti

Ready-to-Read

Simon Spotlight
New York   London   Toronto   Sydney   New Delhi

SIMON SPOTLIGHT
An imprint of Simon & Schuster Children's Publishing Division
1230 Avenue of the Americas, New York, New York 10020
This Simon Spotlight edition July 2018
Text copyright © 2018 by Simon & Schuster, Inc.
Illustrations copyright © 2018 by Valerio Fabbretti
SIMON SPOTLIGHT, READY-TO-READ, and colophon are registered trademarks of Simon & Schuster, Inc.
For information about special discounts for bulk purchases, please contact Simon & Schuster Special Sales at
1-866-506-1949 or business@simonandschuster.com.
Manufactured in the United States of America 0518 LAK
2 4 6 8 10 9 7 5 3 1
This book has been cataloged with the Library of Congress.
ISBN 978-1-5344-1781-6 (hc)
ISBN 978-1-5344-1780-9 (pbk)
ISBN 978-1-5344-1782-3 (eBook)

Contents

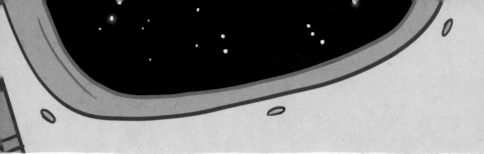

Chapter 1
The Space Race

What comes to mind when you think about space travel? Did you know that some of the biggest advances in space travel came about because of a race between the United States and the Soviet Union? Or that you can't bring a sandwich to the moon, or even onto a space shuttle? Did you know that a group of deaf volunteers helped pave the way for the first American astronauts?

Find out about these stories and more in this book that unlocks the secrets of American history!

The race to space began on October 4, 1957. That was the day the Soviet Union, which was a large country made up of many areas that are now independent countries, including Russia, Ukraine, and Belarus, shocked the world by sending the first man-made satellite (SA-tuh-lite) into space. A satellite is anything that orbits, or circles, a planet or a star. The moon, for example, is a satellite of Earth because it circles the Earth.

The Soviet satellite was called *Sputnik*, which means "fellow traveler." It circled the Earth, sending radio signals back to the Soviet Union.

Today thousands of man-made satellites orbit the Earth. They help us predict the weather, beam television signals and wireless phone calls around the globe, and even take pictures of distant planets.

When *Sputnik* was launched, the United States and the Soviet Union were involved in a conflict called the Cold War. It started after World War II, but even though it was called a war, there were no real battles. Instead, the two countries were cold, or unfriendly, to each other.

The two countries competed to have the best of everything, especially technology and weapons. They sometimes spied on each other to get information. Americans wondered if *Sputnik* would be used to spy on the United States, or even to take control of space. They worried that the powerful rocket used to launch *Sputnik* into space could be used to launch a weapon, too. The United States couldn't let that happen. Suddenly the United States and the Soviet Union were in a race to get to space!

Chapter 2
Secret Satellites

Soon President Eisenhower announced plans for an American satellite. On December 6, 1957, just two months after *Sputnik*, the United States tried to launch a satellite called *Vanguard*, but it exploded three feet from the launchpad. It was such a "flop," or a failure, compared to *Sputnik* that reporters called it *"Flopnik."*

A few months later the United States launched *Explorer 1*, which became the first American satellite to orbit the Earth. They also announced a satellite program, called Discoverer, which they said would be used for a scientific mission.

Discoverer's real name and purpose were actually top secret. It was secretly called Corona, and the program's purpose was to take photos from up in space!

Nowadays digital photos can be sent in an instant over the Internet. In those days most cameras took pictures on rolls of film. The United States needed to find a way to get the film from the Corona program's satellites back to Earth without bringing the satellites home too (so that they could keep taking pictures with a new roll of film). This was achieved in a really cool way!

First, the film was stored inside the cone-shaped front of the Corona satellite. This "nose cone" was also the film's return capsule, a container that kept it safe on the journey! Then, at a specific time and location arranged in advance, the capsule was set up to eject, or detach itself, from the satellite and fall back to Earth.

When it reached about sixty thousand feet above the ground, a parachute attached to the capsule opened. To collect the capsule, an air force unit flew a special plane with circus-style trapeze bars and hooks that they used to snag the capsule's parachute in midair!

If this didn't work, the capsule would land in the ocean, float for a few minutes, and then sink to the bottom to make it hard for an enemy to find it.

Thanks to Corona, the United States had satellite photos of the Soviet Union, and a much clearer idea about the location and number of Soviet weapons.

Corona was so top secret that even though its final launch was in 1972, the American public didn't know about it until 1995.

Chapter 3
The Gallaudet Eleven

The United States finally had a successful satellite program. In 1958, President Eisenhower created a new agency—called the National Aeronautics and Space Administration, or NASA—to advance the space program, but the Soviet Union was still winning the space race. In 1957, they had launched the first dog, named Laika, into space, followed by the first humans a few years later.

Even so, both countries wanted to be the first to reach the moon. The Soviets launched *Luna 1* in January 1959, hoping that the unmanned spacecraft would land on the moon. *Luna 1* missed its target, but it was the first spacecraft to fly beyond the pull of the Earth's gravity. Later that year *Luna 2* reached the moon's surface, and *Luna 3* took pictures of the moon's far side.

Then, in early 1961, John F. Kennedy became president of the United States. He challenged Congress and the American people to put a human on the moon. He said, "I believe that this nation should commit itself to achieving the goal, before this decade is out, of landing a man on the moon and returning him safely to the Earth."

This speech helped support Project Mercury, the first human-in-space program in the United States. Seven military test pilots were already training to become astronauts. In February 1962 astronaut John Glenn became the first American to orbit the Earth. Glenn's spacecraft circled the Earth three times at speeds of more than seventeen thousand miles per hour. After four hours and fifty-six minutes, he landed safely in the Atlantic Ocean.

A mission to the moon would be a much longer journey. Scientists at the US Naval School of Aviation Medicine needed to find out if the human body could handle the intense conditions of space before they let anyone attempt it.

In space flight, astronauts would fly beyond the pull of the Earth's gravity, so their bodies would be weightless. There would also be no horizon line, which is the dividing line between the ground and the sky.

On Earth, when you feel the pull of gravity keeping your feet on the ground and see the horizon line, these observations act as clues that help your body sense which way is up and which way is down. Without these clues, scientists weren't sure if an astronaut would be able to correctly sense his or her body's position in space.

Scientists wanted to test the effects of weightlessness, changes in gravity, and extreme motion on the body. One way they planned to do this was by exposing people to things like spinning rooms and rocking boats for long periods of time.

There was a big problem. Many people get motion sickness—a feeling of being sick to your stomach or dizzy—on bumpy car, plane, or boat rides. Motion sickness is related to balance, which is controlled mainly by the eyes and inner ears. When your eyes and inner ears send conflicting information to the brain, it can cause motion sickness. For example, if your inner ears sense the movement of a rocking boat but you can't see the waves moving, you might feel sick.

Scientists needed to find people who wouldn't get sick . . . even in extreme situations. In 1958, in the early days of the space program, they found the perfect group of volunteers for this research.

A group of eleven volunteers from Gallaudet University, a college for deaf and hard-of-hearing people, participated in testing. Most of them had lost their hearing because of an illness that had damaged their inner ears in a way that made it impossible for them to get motion sickness!

This also meant they could be exposed to weightlessness, changes in gravity, and other situations for longer than most people could without feeling sick at all. This gave scientists time to perform the tests.

The Gallaudet Eleven, as they became known, took part in experiments over the course of ten years to help scientists learn how the human body would react to space travel.

In one test, four of them lived, ate, and slept for twelve days in a circular room that rotated, or turned, ten times per minute.

This helped scientists see how changes in gravity caused by the spinning room affected the volunteers. For one thing, when the volunteers stood, they could tilt their bodies toward the center of the room!

In another test, they were lowered into tubs filled with swirling water, possibly to see how the change in gravity caused by the swirling water would affect them. In yet another, one volunteer rode the elevator in the Empire State Building up and down for hours to test his balance.

They even went on an airplane that had its seats removed to give them room to float inside. The pilot then created around twenty seconds of weightlessness by flying the airplane to the sky and then diving toward the Earth! Since this makes many people feel sick, the plane's nickname is the Vomit Comet!

One time the Gallaudet Eleven were doing a test on board a ship in the already choppy seas of the North Atlantic when a storm hit. While the Gallaudet Eleven were able to continue their card game without getting sick, the ship's crew and scientists got so sick that they had to give up on the experiment!

"We were different in a way they needed," said Harry Larson, one of the volunteers. Without the help of the Gallaudet Eleven, we might not have been able to send a man to the moon.

After learning from the Gaulladet Eleven tests, NASA sent astronauts into space in the Mercury and Gemini programs. Each time, they learned more about space travel and its effects on the body. Finally, on the Apollo 11 mission, they were ready to take humans to the moon and back.

On July 20, 1969, the whole world watched on television as Neil Armstrong, Buzz Aldrin, and Michael Collins landed the Apollo 11 mission's *Saturn V* spacecraft on the moon. As Neil Armstrong stepped onto the surface of the moon, he said words that are famous today: "That's one small step for man, one giant leap for mankind."

The United States had beaten the Soviet Union to the moon!

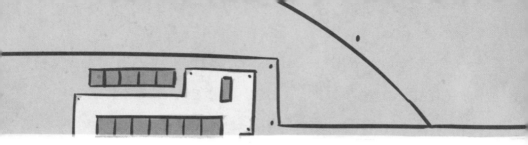

Chapter 4
Food (and Farts!) in Space

Reaching the moon was just the beginning. For the Apollo 11 mission and others, NASA had to figure out how to provide safe food for astronauts to eat. The food had to stay fresh for a long time, be easy to eat in zero gravity, and be packaged in a way that would keep it from flying all over the spacecraft! In the beginning NASA didn't even know if humans could swallow and digest food in an environment without gravity!

John Glenn was the first American to eat in space when he circled the globe. Glenn ate applesauce that had been packed in a flexible tube that looked a lot like a toothpaste tube!

NASA scientists tried other ways to package food too. They covered crumbly or bite-size foods, like strawberry cereal cubes, in a gooey coating called gelatin to keep crumbs from breaking loose.

In space, since there is no gravity to keep a crumb from flying away, it can float into an astronaut's eyes or into the spaceship's instruments. A stray crumb could mean the difference between life and death!

On the Gemini 3 mission, an astronaut named John Young wasn't thinking about crumbs when he surprised Commander Gus Grissom with a treat. He had hidden a corned beef sandwich in his pocket during liftoff and shared it with Grissom. They took a few bites before they realized that crumbs were coming loose from the bread. They were lucky to avoid a disaster!

Food can cause other kinds of problems in space too. During the Apollo program, NASA discovered a change in some astronauts' heartbeats in space. To prevent this, on the Apollo 16 mission NASA added a mineral called potassium (puh-TA-see-yum) to servings of citrus like orange and grapefruit juice. The potassium helped keep the astronauts' heartbeats steady, but it led to another surprising problem—gas!

John Young (the same one who had brought a sandwich to space) was commander of the Apollo 16 mission. He had noticed he was more gassy than usual but hadn't been told why. When he stepped onto the surface of the moon, he told fellow astronaut Charlie Duke that he had "the farts" again and wondered aloud if it was because of all the citrus! He said that as soon as the mission was over, he was never going to eat citrus again!

Young didn't know that his microphone was on and that mission control was listening to their conversation about farts! Even worse, since NASA shared the text of conversations from space missions with the press, some of what Young said about oranges ended up in the news.

The head of an association of Florida citrus growers was furious. He immediately tried to assure the American people that oranges and grapefruits do not cause gas!

That might be one of the funniest things to have happened in space and on Earth!

Thankfully, the Cold War ended in 1991. The different groups that made up the Soviet Union became independent countries. Russia is the biggest of those countries.

In the late 1990s many countries, including Russia and the United States, launched the International Space Station (the ISS). Astronauts from around the world conduct experiments on the ISS to learn about the universe. Even if countries don't always get along on Earth, they are finally working together in space!

Read on to learn more about the secrets of American history, including cool inventions that came about because of the space program, what astronauts ate on the moon, and more!

Space Food Facts

Astronauts don't have to eat just applesauce in space. After trying to package food in tubes, NASA started using a process called freeze-drying to remove 99 percent of the moisture from food.

The freeze-dried food was stored in packets and could stay fresh for a long time. To eat the food inside, astronauts used water guns to inject cold water into the sealed packets. This put water back into the food so that it would taste better. Then the astronauts cut open the packets to eat.

Astronauts on the Project Gemini missions ate shrimp cocktail, chicken and vegetables, and even butterscotch pudding.

On Christmas Eve 1968, NASA surprised the astronauts on *Apollo 8* with a special holiday meal. Meal packets

contained turkey with gravy, and even cranberry sauce that they could eat with a spoon!

What did the Apollo 11 mission's *Saturn V* astronauts eat on the moon? They ate two meals that sound pretty delicious, if a little unusual. The first one included bacon squares, peaches, sugar  cookie cubes, pineapple-grapefruit drink, and coffee. The second meal was beef stew, cream of chicken soup, fruitcake, and grape punch. Not bad!

These days, space food has come a long way. Astronauts traveling to the International Space Station have about 185 different meal choices, ranging from steak to chocolate cake—and everything in between!

Out-of-This-World Inventions

NASA is always inventing new technology for their space missions. But did you know that many of their inventions have also led to exciting products back on Earth? Here are just a few of the everyday items that are made with technology developed for the space program.

Scratch-Resistant Eyeglasses

In the early days of the space program, the clear plastic on space helmet visors could easily be scratched, making it  hard for astronauts to see. A NASA scientist solved the problem by inventing a protective, transparent coating for the visor that makes it much harder to scratch. Today this coating is also used on regular eyeglasses to keep them from getting scratched when they are dropped!

Panoramic Photos

The Mars Exploration Rovers were the first to use a technology that could create a "panoramic" photo. While a regular photo shows a snapshot of a small section of a view, a panoramic photo shows a wider view of the landscape. On Mars, every time a photo was taken, the camera rotated in a full circle to capture each section of the horizon. Then the photos would be arranged side by side to show the full view. The technology is now used in cameras on Earth, and most smartphone cameras can take panoramic photos too!

Swimwear

Space shuttle designers know a lot about drag, a force that slows an object down when it moves through air. Speedo, a swimwear company, adapted NASA's research to create a kind of swimsuit that lowers the drag in the water to help racers swim faster.

Memory Foam

Memory foam was invented in 1966 by NASA researchers to make more comfortable seat cushions for test pilots experiencing bumpy rides. Now it is used in things like

sneakers, mattresses, pillows, helmets, and more!

Moon Artifacts

Perhaps the most famous object on the moon is the American flag, which was planted by astronauts Buzz Aldrin and Neil Armstrong in 1969. But did you know that humans have also left other artifacts behind on the moon? Here are four man-made objects that are still on the moon today.

Gold Olive Branch

On another mission, astronaut Neil Armstrong left a gold olive branch as a symbol of peace.

Golf Balls

Astronaut Alan Shepard hit two golf balls on the moon. Because of the moon's weaker gravity, the balls went soaring and are still there!

Memorial Sculpture

Astronaut David Scott placed a small metal sculpture, titled *Fallen Astronaut*, on the moon along with a plaque. It honors the lives of fourteen astronauts who passed away during active service.

A Family Photo

Astronaut Charlie Duke left a photo of his family on the moon. He sealed it in plastic wrap, probably to keep it free of moondust!

If you could travel to the moon, what object would you leave behind? Would you want to share something personal, like your favorite book, a candy bar, or a photo of your pet? Or would you leave something that relates to the country or the world, like a copy of the US Constitution or an Olympic medal? The possibilities are endless!

YOU CAN'T BRING A SANDWICH TO THE MOON QUIZ

1. What does the word "cold" mean in the Cold War?

a. freezing   b. unfriendly   c. space travel

2. Which astronaut was the first American to orbit the Earth?

a. John Lennon   b. John Young   c. John Glenn

3. What was the name of the first human-made satellite to orbit the Earth?

a. *Sputnik*   b. *Flopnik*   c. *Explorer 1*

4. What were the Gallaudet Eleven unable to suffer from?

a. headaches   b. earaches   c. motion sickness

5. What was the secret purpose of the satellites in the Corona program?

a. a scientific mission   b. to take photos   c. both a and b

6. What kind of container was used in the early space program to hold food?

a. tube   b. suitcase   c. capsule

7. What type of fruit did John Young think made him gassy on the moon?

a. berries   b. citrus   c. mangoes

8. Which of these inventions was first developed by NASA?

a. mattresses   b. helmets   c. memory foam

Answers: 1.b 2.c 3.a 4.c 5.b 6.a 7.b 8.c